PIERO BARGELLINI

THE LITTLE FLOWERS
OF
SAINT CLARE

Translated by
Fr. Edmund O'Gorman, O.F.M. Conv.

Messaggero Editions, Padua, Italy
1972

ACKNOWLEDGEMENT

The Conventual Franciscans of the Messaggero Editions at the Basilica del Santo in Padua, Italy, are indebted to the Friars Minor of the Portiuncula Publications of St. Mary of the Angels in Assisi for granting permission to print this translation.

Price:

U.S.A., Canada and Australia: $ 2.00; United Kingdom, Ireland, Malta and other countries in the Sterling area: 75 p. all other countries, the equivalent of $ 2.00.

CONTENTS

PALM SUNDAY

℘alm Sunday, March 27th, in the year 1211. Clare, with the other young girls and the ladies of Assisi, was at the Cathedral, the old church of San Rufino, where the bishop officiated on these solemn occasions.

The vestments and the hangings were of violet, this being Palm Sunday, the first day of Holy Week, which for the Church is «The Great Week» of the year.

In good time the girls of the town left their homes and headed for the Cathedral for the blessing of the palms. The rocky sides of Mount Subasio reflected the brightness of a timid spring, and some black swifts already flew in and out of the little turrets of the old castle. Of the later castle, the ruins of which still stand, there was no sign, because it was founded only in the year after that of which we speak. The girls had put aside their heavier woolen clothing and dressed themselves in their embroidered and flowered dresses. As they went on their way, their footsteps re-echoed along the narrow flagged streets and stone steps.

Palm Sunday liturgy was long. First came the blessing of the palms, then their distribution; a procession followed, and finally the Mass with the reading of the Passion as written by St. Matthew, during which the people always remained standing.

The ceremony began, «Hosanna to the Son of David. Blessed is He who comes in the name of the Lord: Hosanna in the highest.» It was the liturgical repetition of Our Lord's entry into Jerusalem, riding on an ass. This recalled the great occasion when the men spread their coats and cloaks on the ground before Him like a carpet, and the children broke off branches of palm and olive and, waving them, ran ahead of Him and followed behind shouting that great cry of triumph: «Hosanna!».

After the readings, the responsories, the prayers and the blessing, the bishop began the distribution of the palms: first to the clergy, then to the faithful who kneeling took the palm from the bishop, kissed it, and then kissed his hand. The girls were the last to come up, modest and recollected, their faces slightly hidden under the veils they wore, and under a sort of linen headdress. They approached the celebrant, genuflected, kissed the palm and his hand, and returned quietly to their places.

When Clare's turn came, she did not move. She remained seated with her head bent. She could not quite understand whether she had a feeling of holiness, a sudden bashful impulse, whether she ought to pray or just sit and dream.

In the succession of girls the bishop had noted her absence. He looked towards Clare, but she was not looking at him. Following his gaze went also that of the congregation, somewhat surprised and scandalized.

The bishop's look, however, was not of reproof, rather a certain fatherly understanding. This expressed itself in a rather unusual way for, as though inspired, he rose from his chair, came down the steps of the sanctuary and went up to Clare, who remained unmoved. He presented her with the palm and blessed her, while the whole church followed the incident with astonishment.

Having returned to the altar, the bishop continued with the ceremony. The people sang, «All glory, praise and honour to Thee, Redeemer King,» and the children lovingly joined in with the chorus of «Hosanna!»

Clare, in her seat with the palm branch pressed to her heart, stared ahead of her, still immersed in a sort of stupor.

THE DOOR OF THE DEAD

nearly all of the houses in Assisi had two doors which came onto the street by a step. The ordinary door was large and grandiose with an average sized step, the other was much smaller and narrower with a high step. The two doors, though very near to one another, were not symmetrically placed in the wall because they were of different shapes and at different levels.

To come out from the larger door it was obviously enough to step out as usual, but to use the upper door it was necessary to jump out. While this larger door was nearly always open for people to come and go, the smaller one was customarily kept closed and no one used it. It was called «The Door of the Dead,» because it was opened only to allow the dead to be brought out, feet first, from the house; those who came out this way never returned. According to the custom of those times based in superstition no doubt, it was considered improper for a dead person to be carried from the house through the door used by the living; on the other hand, no living person ever used the Door of the Dead.

So this particular door was kept well bolted until the sad necessity arrived to use it, for if any living person were to pass through — even by mistake — direful misfortune would follow him! Not only was it barred and bolted, but between one funeral and the next all sorts of things were piled up against it.

On that Palm Sunday evening the whole house was asleep when Clare came from her room and tip-toed down towards the Door of the Dead. She wanted to get away secretly, and she was quite sure that she would meet no one on the threshold of that door.

She found the access to the door cluttered up with all sorts of household bits and pieces, which she slowly and quietly removed, a type of work which she was quite unaccustomed to, so that when she arrived at the door itself, she felt just a little bit tired. She tried hard to move the bolts, but they had rusted in their sockets, for the door had not been opened since her father died and his body was carried through.

Clare knelt down, with her hands on the lower bolt of the door, and said a prayer. She rose from her knees, strengthened in her resolve to go ahead. Once more she tugged at the bolts, and this time, slowly, slowly, they slid across. The door opened bit by bit with hardly a creak or a crackle. Below was the street reflecting the moonlight, and there also in a corner, under cover of the darkness, was her faithful friend, Pacifica di Guelfuccio.

Clare paused for a minute on the threshold, and then, without looking behind, she landed with a light jump onto the street. She had crossed through the Door of the Dead. She was now irrevocably separated from her family. Never again would she be able to return to her house. Clare was lost: Clare was dead! Clare had passed over to another life!

THE HOSTAGE OF HEAVEN

Our Lady of the Angels is so called because, it is said, four pilgrims passing by that spot heard the songs of angels. There was a very little chapel, the meeting place for St. Francis' first companions. It stood in a wood in the plain below Assisi.

The whole area, woods and little church, was a small piece of land that belonged to the Benedictine Abbot of Mount Subasio. It was called «Portiuncula,» the very little, neglected piece, in contrast to the large estates of the Abbey which the monks had planted with trees and developed.

Francis with his own hands had repaired this ruined little church, and then with his companions built a few small cabins or huts of brushwood in the shade of the woods. He paid a rent every year to the Benedictines — a wicker-basket of fish, which the friars got from the nearby brook Tescio.

During the day when the friars were out working or preaching, St. Mary of the Angels was deserted, but at night it was all lit up with pine-torches and resounded with the praises of Our Lady.

And indeed, brighter than ever it was on that Sunday night when Clare, accompanied by Pacifica di Guelfuccio, came down towards it

from Assisi. Waiting for her at the edge of the
woods were Philip and Bernard with lighted
torches. Still clad in their feast-day dresses, the
girls followed the silent friars along the woodland path. The briars pulled and caught at their
dresses, and it seemed as if invisible hands were
trying to impede their progress through the
woods. A few night birds, frightened by the
torches, flitted across in front of the two
fugitives.

At the door of the tiny chapel Francis
waited, his facial lines furrowed by the shade
and his eyes smarting from the smoke of burning pine-wood and lack of sleep: he looked out
at Clare, who came forward and knelt before
him. On each side of him were other bearded
friars in their habits.

A passing stranger might have fled from
this sight as a scene of brigandage; he might
have thought the two girls had fallen into a den
of robbers. Apparently eager hands took jewels
and precious ornaments from Clare; they divested her of her wonderfully embroidered
dress and took off her feet the little shoes of
satin. They then put a coarse habit over her and
fastened it round her waist with a rope.

Dressed in this way in her bare feet, they then led her into the gothic chapel. St. Mary of the Angels was splendid with sprays and branches of broom, but much of this woodland beauty was lost in the red light of the torches and in the smoke that came from them.

Like one condemned to death they led her on her knees to the foot of the altar. Francis took a razor and approached Clare. He knew what was customary to do. The young girl's tresses, fresher and yellower than the broom, fell to the steps of the altar, and Francis placed on her shorn head a rough piece of woollen cloth.

And while she was thus being divested of all her worldly beauty, the friars in their rough habits and unshorn heads chanted forth, as was the custom, the Office of the Dead for a young lady stolen from the world and made a hostage of heaven.

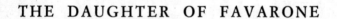

THE DAUGHTER OF FAVARONE

Clare was eighteen years old. Francis thirty. Clare came from a noble family, Francis from a family of merchants.

At Assisi you could count the noble families on the fingers of one hand. There were the Compagnani, the Tibaldi, the Corani, the Ghislerio, the Fiumi, from which house came Madonna Ortolana, the mother of Clare. For a long time they thought the surname of Clare's father was Scifi, but we only know that he was called Favarone di Offreduzzo. He died and left five women at home — wife Ortolana, and the four daughters, Penenda, Clare, Agnes and Beatrice; although all of them were marriageable, however, not all were of the age for marriage.

In those times girls were 'promised out' even as babies, as someone grumbled, «They were married in the cradle!» This in fact was fairly correct, for there were cases of children marrying at twelve, fourteen and sixteen years of age. Indeed, after sixteen mothers began to fear for the future of their daughters: they were then thought of already as spinsters!

Customarily, it was not the girl herself who chose her lover. This was thought out by the parents, who promised her, not indeed to the boy, but to the boy's parents. Such promises made for a baby girl were sometimes celebrated as actual espousals when the girl was about four years old. Parents seeking their future sons-in-law took count of the condition of the family, the good standing of the parents, the richness of the household, and blue-bloodedness.

Then they did their best to arouse love between the two, speaking well of the boy to the girl, and vice-versa, and arranging get-togethers for them at festivals in the town. For the most part, love matches arranged in this way usually turned out well, just as fire is rekindled by the timely stirring of the embers.

Clare had been spoken to many times in this way, with hints at the eligible young noblemen in the town, but she always let the question drop. She seemed more interested in hearing news about that strange type of individual, the merchant. These belonged to a different group from the nobility; usually they were intelligent and enterprising, but men of lower birth and somewhat looked down on.

They owed their fortunes to business ability. Instead of complaining of their misfortunes together in front of their craft workshops, they went forth on risky journeys to buy and sell in far-away markets, away from their town,

outside the limits of their Commune, beyond
their own regions, even beyond the mountains
and as far away as France and Flanders. There
was always the danger of returning with hardly
any merchandise — or even of not returning
at all — because of brigands robbing the mule
caravans. But if everything went well and luck
was with them, a fortune was made overnight.
Such adventurous men were referred to as «The
Great Merchants.»

Pietro di Bernardone was one of these. He
had changed his son's name from John to Francis, that is «French,» in memory of his suc-
cessful trading in France. At the beginning the
nobles of Assisi had looked down on these newly
rich merchants. Gradually, the glitter of gold
began to diminish the pretentions of the nobility.
Francis, for example, was accepted among them
as an equal, until the day came when the
merchant's son preferred the company of the
lepers to that of the gentlemen.

The whole Assisi was speaking about the
strange sort of life Francis was leading. Clare,
too, felt involved. She wanted to know more
about him and his way of life. So she went out
of her way to meet him; and, walking one day

with a companion, Bona di Guelfuccio, she accosted him coming from the town. While the rest ran away, she spoke with him.

Francis gazed at the young Clare as one would gaze at a star. He said:

«You will have to know how to die.»

«What do you mean?» enquired Clare.

«On the Cross with Christ.»

And so when that Palm Sunday began and the Passion of Our Lord was being read, among the Hosannas of the liturgy, Clare decided from that moment to die as Francis had advised her.

UNCLE MONALDO

Madonna Ortolana was a widow with four marriageable daughters. But she did not stand alone. The brothers of her dead husband, the children's uncles, were very close to her, especially Monaldo, the oldest and most authoritative.

These uncles, with Monaldo at their head, took it as their duty to see the girls made good marriages. Their family was noble, and noble and rich must the young men be who would take the daughters of Favarone. Although they were fatherless, there were no girls in Assisi better watched over than Penenda, Clare, Agnes and Beatrice. Uncles and cousins continually kept their eyes on them.

So when Monaldo heard that Clare had run away, it was as though the sight vanished from his eyes, as though he had been struck by his worst enemy in the middle of the town square! That rascal Francis! Not content with having robbed his own father, he now robbed the Favarone household. Having dishonoured the merchant, he was now bent on dishonouring the nobility. Having impoverished Bernard, he was now ruining Clare!

Monaldo called all the relations to arms. There was no time to lose, and it was not yet high noon before they converged in the woods encircling the Portiuncula. However, Clare was no longer there; for, after having cut her hair, Francis had confided her to the care of the nuns of St. Paul.

A nun's convent was like a fortress. No one could enter even by force. Monaldo threatened and shouted. Seeing that a violent attitude was getting him nowhere, he changed his tone, seeking to gain the confidence of his niece. Through an intermediary he asked her to think of the great sorrow her flight had caused her mother, and the harm that could come to her sisters because of it. But it all fell flat, for the promises were mere words.

He then sought to speak with her himself. Clare agreed, but chose the church as the meeting place. Near to the altar she would feel safer. Monaldo, the relations and the servants left their weapons outside the church and entered. They tried to cover their indignation with a cloak of meekness, genuflected before the altar, made the Sign of the Cross, and got up when they saw her coming through the choir.

She came forward quickly, went up the steps of the altar and with her right hand grasped the white altar cloth. This was the gesture of all those who, in those days of violence, sought the right of asylum in the church. Just as a baby feels secure when it can clasp in its tiny hands the clothing of its mother, so the fugitive and the persecuted not only felt, but actually was, safe when she was able to fly to the bosom of Mother Church as represented by the altar cloth. No power on earth would have been able to drag Clare away from that right she claimed.

Monaldo and the other relations well understood Clare's action: but, at least, might he have a word with her?

Still holding the altar cloth with her right hand, she raised her left hand and took the black veil from her head. A shocked pang of sorrow hit them all when they saw that her blond tresses were no more. Clare looked at them all for a few seconds as though waiting to be admired; she replaced the black veil over her head and face, let go the altar cloth, and disappeared back into the shadows of the cloister.

SISTER AGNES

The convent where St. Francis had at first placed Clare was that of St. Paul. After a few days he transferred her from there and placed her in the monastery of the nuns of Sant'Angelo di Panzo on the hillside of Mount Subasio.

Each day Clare's younger sister Agnes went up there to visit her. One evening she did not return home to the family, but sent word that she, too, intended to stay at the convent. Once again, in great anger, Uncle Monaldo took to the road. Clare, after all, was eighteen; but Agnes was hardly fifteen and was still under parental authority. Yes, he would go with an escort of armed servants and get her. Indeed, they found her and with thumps and blows forced her away with them, as she shouted for help:

«Clare, my sister, help me!»

Clare did not move a finger. She was praying, and it seemed to her then that what was happening outside the convent to her sister was not all that important.

Agnes' captors took the short cut through the woods full of stones and bushes. They dragged her away furiously over the stones and through the bushes, so that every stone was reddened by her blood and every thorn-hedge plucked a blond hair from her head. They were so rough and brutal with her, that after a short way she fell to the ground with fatigue and mistreatment. Monaldo gave orders that she should be picked up and carried.

The strong men stooped down to lift her, but their arms seemed to lack strength.

«It seems that she's been eating lead all night,» they said, straightening out their aching backs.

In fact, Agnes' body became even heavier than lead and seemed to be part of the very earth on which she lay!

Monaldo, beside himself with rage, lifted his arm to strike at his niece with a clenched fist, but his arm stuck paralysed in the air!

He roared with pain that tormented him in his arm. His followers, frightened by the punishment they had seen, fled through the countryside. Even Uncle Monaldo, screaming from pain, ran back to Assisi. Agnes remained as though dead, among the thorns and stones, abandoned by all.

But see—Clare then left her convent. She followed the bloodstained stones and golden locks on the bushes to the place where her sister was lying. Gently, she took her by the hand.

«Get up, Agnes, and let us go together to serve our Divine Spouse, Jesus Christ.»

Agnes got to her feet, clean and fresh as though nothing had ever happened, as though she were simply rising to a very beautiful and glorious morning.

THE LADY POVERTY

A little while afterwards, St. Francis took Clare and her followers from the Benedictine convent of Sant'Angelo with the intention of placing them in St. Damian's.

It was in this half ruined church that the Crucifix had spoken to Francis: «Francis, go and repair my Church which is falling into ruins.» At the time the young man understood the command to apply to the material building, and so with stones and mortar he repaired it. Later he came to see that the command of Christ meant something else, that the Church was to be taken as the Mystical Body of Christ suffering on the Cross.

He renounced his riches, gave up every worldly ambition and became of his own wish, humble and poor. As he put it, he espoused the Lady Poverty.

Even after the sufficient but inexpert repair work done by Francis, St. Damian's still remained a very poor place. It was like the church of St. Mary of the Angels, small and dark with an ogival vault. The construction around the church could surely be adapted for a convent for a few ladies, especially for the «Poor Ladies.» And so at St. Damian's was born the Second Franciscan Order, for women, that had been called the «Poor Ladies.» «Poor Ladies»

— that was enough. No other designation was necessary: poor ladies who lived on alms, ate the bread of beggars, and consequently fasted more often than they ate.

Francis had freely embraced poverty. Clare wished to be poverty itself, poverty in person. In this sense she became one with Francis, in strictest poverty, sought and accepted, followed for the love of that great poor Man, the Master and Lord of the Universe, Jesus.

This old church, with its great crucifix, was decorated with masses of wild flowers. In the apse were the choir stalls of the «Poor Ladies,» made of coarse unplaned wood. Fixed into the paving stones was a post that supported a small lectern lit by an oil lamp. An iron grille separated the nuns from the church, and through this grille they received Holy Communion. Through a little cloister constructed of pilasters without capitals, one entered the refectory, narrow and dim, with rough wooden tables ranged round the walls and no tablecloths. Here, with thanks to the good Lord, the Poor Ladies ate whatever they were able to beg. Clare preferred pieces of bread: to her a whole loaf seemed far too rich. They asked for what was thrown away and lived on leftovers. A whole loaf came as a great gift.

Upstairs there was only one room where the Poor Ladies gathered: a largish room, bare and cold under the rafters of the roof. The bed was nothing but a bundle of twigs, with a piece of wood serving as a pillow and bedsheets of rough hemp and covers of patches sewn together.

In every season of the year the Ladies went barefooted, clad in a coarse dress girded at the waist with a rope. Over their shorn heads they wore a white head cloth and a black veil on top. Clare under her clothing wore also a hair shirt made of pig skin with the rough side inwards.

«Poor Ladies» indeed! It was impossible to be poorer than they. At St. Damian's Clare wished that there should be the very primacy of poverty. There was to be nowhere else in the whole world a lady poorer than she: nothing was hers, everything was borrowed, simply lent to her.

Voluntary poverty was not only accepted, but sought after as the greatest of privileges; a happy poverty contented in itself, a sort of festive poverty with nothing repugnant or sorrowful about it, a poverty, indeed, full of thorns, but flowering like roses, smiling and joyous under the influence of grace.

From St. Damian's there were no laments and no sighs. The poverty of that small place caused no sorrow, the meanness of their table caused no complaints, the discomfort of those beds of twigs was not a source of torment. Clare wanted to be poverty itself. The poorer she became, the happier she was.

THE MEAL IN THE WOODS

Francis came and went from St. Mary of the Angels, but Clare found herself like a prisoner at St. Damian's. She knew that in seeking always to become poorer she had not taken a wrong turn. Often she longed to speak with Francis, to whom she looked as to a father for support.

When she had heard that Francis, having returned from his journeyings, was at St. Mary's, she sent word that she would like to see him at St. Damian's. On the other hand, Francis stayed well away from the convent, for he did not wish that the common people should take scandal from seeing him going frequently in and out.

There was one particular occasion when Clare felt a great desire to have a meal with Francis. Surely, there are no friends and relations who do not wish to have a meal together now and again. Taking food is, in a certain way, a humiliating experience that even the most spiritual of men have in common with the brute creation. However, when food is taken together and shared, it then becomes an act of charity and spirituality.

Our Lord himself accepted an invitation to eat, even with publicans. To all his followers

He has left himself under the form of bread at the Eucharistic table.

Therefore, Clare very much wanted to have a meal with Francis, at least once. But Francis always avoided the occasion.

The brothers were sorry for Clare, and they spoke about it to Francis in a rather reproving way.

«Father,» they said, «it does not seem to us that your way of acting accords very well with charity. Clare has given up all the riches of the world; she is a choice plant in your spiritual garden. Why then do you not wish to make her happy in so little a thing as allowing her to have a meal with you?»

Francis knew in his heart that he was being too strict, and he was pleased to have this advice of his friends. He was afraid lest sympathy for Clare might disturb his judgement. He asked them:

«Do you think I ought to listen to her?»

«Yes, indeed, Father. Clare deserves this and other considerations as well.»

«If it seems that way to you, then it seems that way also to me.»

Still, he would not go to St. Damian's.

Instead, he sent an invitation to Clare to come to Our Lady of the Angels.

«She has been a long time at St. Damian's,» Francis said with the tenderness of a true Father. «She will be happy to come out for a little while and to see in the daytime that place to which she first came at night, where her hair was cut from her, and where she was received among us. In the name of Jesus Christ, we will picnic in the woods.»

And so at last Clare came to the Portiuncula. First she prayed on her knees at the altar of Our Lady. Afterwards Francis showed her round, pointing out the little huts in the shadows of the trees. In her bare feet Clare followed him round the stony pathways and noted the low hedges that formed the limits of the friary. At the side of a little brook she stopped. Nearby they found a clean surfaced stone, and there they sat down on the grass while Clare's companion and one of the brothers served them both with crusts of bread and cups of fresh water. The sun flickered through the trees as the branches swayed in the breeze. Overhead the birds were celebrating with their spring songs.

However, before placing any food to his

mouth, Francis began to speak of the Lord and His charity and love. This love of which Francis spoke became like a flame of fire, which from the first utterance entered the souls of those who were present and sent them into ecstasy. This light spread to the woods with such brilliance that the sun was overshadowed. The Portiuncula became one great mass of light. From Assisi it seemed as though the woods were on fire.

From far away people came running to put out the flames. As they neared the place they could see that there was nothing burning in the woods, which nevertheless was full of light. Approaching close to where the light shone brightest, the people found Clare and Francis with their companions seated near the stone table and rapt in ecstasy, enveloped in a halo of an immaterial glow. The very woods seemed wonder-struck and still, even the larks were spellbound and quiet upon its branches.

Slowly the brightness diminished as the spiritual fire spent itself. The crowd that had gathered went away slowly and respectfully. Trees began to move again in the breeze, the brook babbled, and the larks flew freely.

Finally, Clare and Francis with their two helpers rose from the ground, overjoyed and filled with spiritual nourishment, not having touched as much as a crumb of the material food.

A KISS FOR THE SERVANT

$\mathcal{B}$ack at St. Damian's Clare continued to shed light around her. Her friends from the town came to visit her. To them she repeated the words of St. Francis: Poverty places everything beneath its feet, and in this way it is queen of all things.

There were many who stayed at St. Damian's with her. Pacifica di Guelfuccio, who was Clare's companion on that Palm Sunday night when she fled to the Portiuncula, remained there. She had returned to the town, but from that night on she had no peace until she came and joined Clare and Agnes.

Then came the turn of two other very young girls, Benvenuta and Filippa, daughters of Leonardo di Gislerio. They, too, were noble and rich, and quite pretty. Following them came others: Illuminata, Angeluccia, Cristiana, Lucia, Benedetta, and Beatrice.

All the better class families of Assisi lived in constant worry, for the most loved girls could not resist the call of St. Damian's. They were happy to give away their dowries to the poor, they went barefooted, allowed their hair to be clipped away by scissors, and enclosed themselves in this little convent.

There, in a state of the strictest poverty, they discovered the happiness that they had sought for in vain at banquets. They found the peace which they could not find in the world. There they felt happy. They lived as 'sisters,' and used that word to one another without any envy or jealousy.

Francis· had called them «The Poor Ladies,» but the people were already calling them by other names: 'Damianites,' and 'Clares.' Clare was, in fact, their guide. From her came a good example in everything.

At one time Francis had wished that even the Poor Ladies should have their Rule of Life written out for them, and Clare should take the authority of abbess. For three years, feeling that she was too young, she refused to be their superior. When she reached twenty-one, she gave way. She found a way of changing her authority into greater sacrifice.

Clare made herself the servant of the sisters at the table and in the dormitory, and as a servant she was up before others, sweeping and washing. The most humiliating and repugnant work she considered as especially hers. She took great care of the sick and sat with the gravely ill through the night.

She considered that her great privilege as

a superior was to work the hardest and to eat the least. When alms was very scarce, she made it a matter of obedience that the sisters should eat every crust, while she herself fasted.

One of her privileges was to wash the feet of those who went about like the servants of the rest, attending to the external affairs of the convent. When they returned with their bare feet either muddy or dusty, Clare would be waiting for them with a basin and a towel, and kneeling down before them she washed them and kissed each instep. One day one of them, feeling that Clare ought not to be doing this menial service, withdrew her foot just as the Abbess was about to kiss it, and inadvertently she kicked the superior in the mouth.

A trickle of blood appeared between Clare's lips, and the pain filled her eyes with tears. The offender apologized profusely and wanted to get to her knees, but Clare smiled in spite of her tears, raised her gently up, and this time kissed the callous soles of her feet.

THE ROSES

Clare would have liked to have seen Francis frequently. There were so many things that she wanted to ask him! She could manage with very little material food, but she required much more of that spiritual nourishment which came from the words of the master.

On the other hand, Francis kept himself well away from St. Damian's. He remarked to his brothers:

«Beware of the poison of familiarity with women!»

Clare could not be thought of as poison, nor could she be a source of temptation to Francis, a most penitential man. But Francis wanted to set an example for the rest, keeping himself from the first away from St. Damian's and avoiding conversation with the «Poor Ladies.»

Clare was saddened by this, and her sorrow came to the ears of Francis.

«Do not think,» he answered, «that I do not love them with a perfect love. I only wish to give you an example that I want you to imitate.»

Certainly he loved them all, these «Poor Ladies» who followed his teaching. Above all, he loved Clare and prayed for her that she might remain faithful to Christ and to the ideal of poverty. Clare was his masterpiece. She was the most splendid star in the sky, but like a star, she was to be admired from a distance.

Still, Clare had a need, especially in those early years, of guidance. She was afraid she did not know enough alone to lead her sisters in the perfect way of poverty: that was why she looked for a visit from the master.

From time to time Francis did visit her, but his appearances at St. Damian's were momentary. He knocked at the door and greeted them: «Peace and good-will.» He glanced inside and noted that the convent was «a strong tower of sovereign poverty.» Nothing useless or purposeless, nothing sumptuous or superfluous.

Neither was there anything squalid or sad about the place, a clean and serene poverty with joy everywhere. All was clear where Clare was; all was gracious where was the grace of God.

One cold winter's day Francis stood, ready to leave, as he had come, without having accepted any other comfort than the knowledge that true poverty was being observed and that all the young nuns were perfectly happy in their life.

So he walked toward the door. Outside the wind whistled and blew through the branches of the olive trees, and snow was settling in little droves and sleet was forming upon the front pathway. Francis' bare feet stepped out onto the snow and Clare followed after him a few paces away. She hoped to detain him a little. At least she hoped to get a promise from him of another visit very soon.

Francis pulled his hood up over his head:

«Sister Clare,» he said, «it is better that we go our own ways, because of what the world might think. I will leave you to manage on your own.»

Clare, standing in the brightness of the ground, felt lost and astray:

«What will I do without you? You are my guide and support.»

Francis raised his eyes to the somber sky:

«Our Blessed Lord will guide you.»

«And we will not see you again?»

Francis looked about. Considering the weather conditions and seeing a thorny rosebush covered with snow, he said to Clare:

«We will meet again when the roses reflower.»

It was the beginning of winter, and the roses would not flower again until well into the spring. He wanted to place a complete season between himself and Clare.

«Let it be as you wish,» answered Clare, «but also as Our Lord wishes.» And she bowed her head.

Francis made to move away, but almost immediately he involuntarily stopped. On the bush that was near him suddenly and miraculously groups of roses had flowered!

Clare, under her double veil, smiled to herself; and when Francis had gone off towards Spello in the snowstorm, she went back into St. Damian's with a bunch of roses in her hands which she placed at the feet of the Crucifix.

ORTOLANA

Ortolana dei Fiumi, the widow of Favarone, had planned that each of her daughters should have a grand wedding.

In her large palace of Subasio stone, which was her home, she had gathered a chest full of linen and Umbrian embroidery; in another chest, sprinkled with pepper against moths, she had the softest woolen cloth, bought from the store of Pietro di Bernardone.

But now her daughters one after the other had left their home to follow the example of Clare. She was left alone, the sole guardian of all this useless splendour. Clare, Agnes and Beatrice had chosen treasures which rust could not destroy nor moth consume.

These chests of precious clothing seemed like coffins in her house, while down at St. Damian's where there was strictest poverty, she knew the place was alive with holiness.

And so, one day even the widow of Favarone gave away to the needy all those riches she had so jealously gathered about her. She renounced her social standing and in her bare feet went out through the gate of her palace and abandoned everything. Down through the groves of olives she went, and eventually knocked at the door of St. Damian's and asked her own daughter to accept her — as a spiritual daughter.

Thus Clare became the Mother Superior of her own mother: a mother attentive and serving, and like the others, inflexible in observing the Rule. Ortolana, for all her age, was like an awkward child before Clare. In the world she had developed habits and preconceived ideas that from time to time showed under the veil, but Clare sweetly watched over her lest the pride and ambition of a Lady of Means should again begin to show itself in her.

Adjoining the convent there was a piece of land concerning which the Rule said: «That land is not to be cultivated in any other way but for the needs of the sisters.» Ortolana was assigned to cultivate that little garden; she who in the world was named 'Ortolana,' became 'ortolana' in fact (Note: the word in Italian means «a lady gardener»). Her delicate and aristocratic hands very soon became quite rough, and her face reflected the coarseness of the weather; but as the plant flowers among the furrows in the soil, so through her wrinkles flowered the happiness of a soul finally at peace.

Occasionally Ortolana was worried because a young plant was killed by the frost or because the wind broke off a branch, but Clare taught her to trust in Divine Providence.

In the garden the miracle of creation was constantly renewing itself and in the convent other miracles happened because of the absolute reliance of Clare on Our Blessed Lord.

One day when the hour for supper had already passed, it was found that there was only one piece of bread in the whole house. The sister in charge of the refectory was hesitant in ringing the bell, and Clare summoned her in order to know the reason for the delay.

«We will have to fast this evening,» said the sister; «we have only one loaf of bread. And besides, there are two beggars standing at the door.»

«Go, my daughter, and break it into pieces,» said Clare; «give half to the beggars, and of the other half make pieces for all of us sisters.»

«How on earth is it possible to break such bread into so many small pieces?» asked the sister; «there would not be even one piece for everyone.»

But Clare, sure of herself, repeated the order:

«Go, my daughter; go, and do as I say, and have full trust in the Providence of God.»

And while the refectorian dealt with the bread, Clare prayed; and the bread increased, becoming enough to feed the whole convent!

There were always a few brothers chosen from the most reliable of the brethren, sent by St. Francis, who were ready to go begging for alms for the sisters. The most gallant of these was Brother Bentivenga. One day he appeared at the garden wall and enquired if the sisters needed anything. Ortolana, who was there, said to him:

«We have no oil.»

«Make the container ready,» he said, «and place it on the wall. I will pass later, and take it».

However, it was Clare herself who prepared the container, cleaning it out with cinders and boiling water. She then put it up on the wall. Brother Bentivenga, passing by later, saw it, and was about to take it down but found that it was much heavier than usual. He looked inside. The large jug was full of the finest, clearest oil with a small green olive leaf floating on the surface!

THE CIRCLE OF ASHES

Clare was insistent that Francis should visit the Poor Ladies of St. Damian's more often. Her convent was a stronghold of humility, poverty and chastity. The three Franciscan vows were kept in the very strictest manner at St. Damian's. The fidelity of Clare to Francis consisted in the perfect and willing observance of those three vows, which formed the most intimate part of their lives.

Francis knew this. He was well acquainted with Clare's integrity, and he looked on her as the living image of his gospel ideal. There could be no one so capable of extreme sacrifices and total dedication as a woman. This woman was Clare.

From the moment when the daughter of Ortolana had shaken off the trammels of her own house, she had had no uncertainty and no regrets. Securely and quickly she moved along the way of perfection that Francis had pointed out to her.

Francis understood this and was happy about it, but Clare would have wished for more guidance and instruction from him; she wanted spiritual assistance. Any lack of bread did not disconcert her, and that of wine less so; the jar of oil which Brother Bentivenga watched over on

the wall was kept full either by benefactors or
by the charity of Our Lord.

She, therefore, felt the need of few words;
she suffered from a lack of constant spiritual
help.

On the other hand, Francis was prepared
to leave her more alone than ever with her
penance and prayer, to leave her completely in
the hands of God. Her ties with the world she
had broken and he felt she was able to rest
securely anchored to the immense and tranquil
bosom of Divine Providence.

He not only stopped visiting Clare himself,
but he influenced the brothers also to give their
spiritual assistance less frequently to the Ladies
at St. Damian's. Brother Bentivenga indeed appeared at the wall of the convent, but only to
enquire as to what things the Poor Ladies needed
for their material well-being. Ortolana was always ready to hand him the basket for bread
and the jar for oil, until one day Clare made up
her mind that she would receive nothing else
from them:

«If we are going to be deprived of our
spiritual nourishment,» she said firmly but without resentment, «we will be able to manage also

without their material help.»

The stronghold of sovereign poverty thus raised the last drawbridge linking the world.

Francis was not slow to grasp the significance of Clare's words. From him she and her companions were waiting for a lesson on the spiritual life. They wanted to hear from his own lips one of those discourses that so fired the soul. Perhaps they had hoped that he would renew, there among the olive groves round St. Damian's, that prodigy of the mystical fire in the woods at St. Mary of the Angels.

Therefore, he set out along the road that leads from St. Mary's up to St. Damian's. He knocked at the door of the convent.

The news spread quickly among them that their Father had finally given in and had arrived among them, and the Poor Ladies eagerly crowded around him.

Francis, silent and absentminded, made as if to meditate, and Clare intimated that they should all sit round and be ready to listen. After some time the voice of the Father uttered words that pierced to the marrow of their bones.

He was not a gifted orator: his language, especially at the start, was somewhat hesitant.

As his fervour increased, he shifted from foot to foot as though he were standing on hot bricks. His discourses were short and his words full of pain. Only when he pronounced the holy Name of Jesus did his voice take on an extraordinary sweetness; he passed his tongue over his lips as though that word had the taste of honey.

In the silence of St. Damian's Clare waited, expecting the words to come forth from Francis in an uncontrollable torrent. Instead, Francis was silent, absorbed in other things; he was quite prepared to await the inspiration from on high. That inspiration was not slow in coming.

As if stirring from meditation, he asked them to bring him some ashes. With these he made a circle around himself on the floor, sprinkled some on his head, and then in a most sorrowful voice, he intoned the 'Miserere';

Have mercy upon me, O God, in your kindness, in your compasssion, blot out mine offence.
Wash me more and more from my guilt, and cleanse me from my sin.

As his singing of the penitential psalm came to its end, Francis left the circle of ashes and quickly went away from the convent.

THE FACE IN THE WELL

Clare understood the lesson. Even Francis was nothing else but ashes. And she too was ashes, even though pure and chaste. Spiritual pride could be the ruin of the penitents' souls, and could take all love for God from their hearts.

Chanting the 'Miserere,' Francis had revealed his misery and his weakness. Even the strongest and noblest person could do nothing without the help of the Saviour.

Prayer was, therefore, very necessary, for pride which was dispelled so far as material and worldly things were concerned was, nevertheless, well ready to return and attack the soul and its intimate spirituality. Clare prayed. She prayed the canonical hours in choir. She prayed when she worked, she prayed eating. From her hard bed during the night she rose, knelt down and prayed. This constantly intense prayer reflected itself on her face, as one of her companions had left on record: «When she returned after praying her face seemed clearer and more resplendent than the sun.»

This was what St. Francis desired. Though far away from St. Damian's, he thought of Clare and her Poor Ladies. He was afraid lest their shining example should be hidden and their splendour obscured.

For he knew very well that it is not enough to have renounced the world. One must likewise renounce Satan. And especially Satan because he is pride personified.

Besides the two Franciscan vows of poverty and chastity, there was also that humility, which followed on the other two as a necessary consequence and could not be maintained or strengthened unless by constant and sincere prayer.

For this reason St. Francis at St. Damian's chanted the 'Miserere,' the prayer of humility and penance:

My offences truly I know them; my sin is always before me.

Against you, you alone, have I sinned; what is evil in your sight, I have done.

After that lesson of the ashes, Clare increased her penances and intensified her prayers.

Far from her Francis prayed that her light might shine ever clearer before men. Standing in prayer during the night, he raised his eyes to the stars and asked the Lord to let the Poor Ladies shine with splendour even as those heavenly bodies. But the sky was a long way off and perhaps it was presumptuous to look up so far,

Francis would receive his confirmation of Clare's humility and purity by looking down.

One night when there was a full moon, he was out on a long journey with Brother Leo, 'The Little Sheep of God,' and they arrived, tired and dusty, at an open well. Francis went up to it and for a long time stood there gazing down into the darkened shaft of the well as though attracted by something in the water below. When he went away from the parapet, he seemed in a state of ecstasy; he had not even asked for a drink, but continued walking, singing and praising the Lord.

After a while, as though sensing the perplexity of Brother Leo who was walking behind him, he stopped and asked his companion:

«Brother Leo, what do you think I saw reflected on the water down in that well?»

«My Father,» said Brother Leo, «you would have seen the moon that was shining in the sky.»

«No,» Brother Leo, «I saw there the face of our Sister Clare who I thought was suffering and under temptation. Instead, she was all peace and brightness. Because of this my heart is now set at peace in her regard, and full of joy and gratitude to my Saviour.»

Clare in her humility and her prayer became ever more perfect. Francis could well say:

«After God and His heavens — Clare!»

THE WILL OF GOD

E rancis was accustomed to go to Clare for counsel and advice. She was a source of such enlightenment that Francis saw in her a reflexion of the Divine Wisdom. As the moon receives the glory of its brightness from the sun, so Clare received her splendour from the grace of God.

Whenever Francis wanted to know what was the will of God, he always asked the Sister at St. Damian's.

From the start of his conversion, the saint had been torn between the desire of contemplation and the duty of preaching.

«Does the good Lord wish me to be a hermit or a missionary? Should I dedicate myself to a life of prayer in the woods and among the rocky hillsides, or ought I to preach in the squares and the towns? Does He call me to the contemplative life or the active life?»

Now and then this doubt tormented him, in the solitude of the woods where he felt the need and the sweetness of contemplation as well as in the company of men where he felt the satisfaction of spending himself in charity for their salvation.

To settle this doubt once for all and to clear it up, he wanted a definite sign of what the will of God was in his regard. Francis could, indeed, have asked this directly from God; but, instead, he had recourse to Clare. She was a sure messenger of the Will of the Lord.

Francis called Brother Masseo to himself and said:

«Go along to Sister Clare and ask her to gather together her more spiritual nuns and to pray that the Lord might reveal to them what is better for me: to preach or to pray. Then, go along to Brother Sylvester and tell him the same thing.»

Brother Sylvester was the first priest among the friars and lived like a hermit near a large canal of Mount Subasio. Because of this Francis held him in great respect.

Brother Masseo therefore went to St. Damian's and made his message known to Clare, who gathered her companions together in prayer before that same crucifix which had spoken to Francis.

Then Masseo went off towards Subasio in search of Sylvester. The first Franciscan priest had already had a vision from which he was easily able to deduce what was to be Francis' work. For instance, one day while he was praying, he saw a cross of gold come from the mouth of Francis. The cross became bigger and bigger until it embraced the whole world and reached to heaven. To him this meant that the preaching of Francis would go out over the whole world, leading all men to heaven.

The answer of Sylvester was crystal clear:

«This is what God says, and you are to tell Fr. Francis: The Lord has not called you for yourself but also for the souls that will be saved through you.»

Brother Masseo came down from the mountain and back to St. Damian's. Clare also had received an answer, and it was the same as Sylvester's:

«Tell Francis that God wishes him to preach in the world.»

When the brother eventually returned to the Portiuncula, Francis was much concerned about him after so long a journey. He washed his feet, dirty after the walk, generally assisted him, prepared the table for a meal, and then in great humility served him.

After the meal he took Brother Masseo to a quiet place out in the woods. There he knelt down before him, drew his hood over his head, extended his arms in the form of a cross, and without seeking the answer of Clare or Sylvester, simply asked:

«What command did my Saviour Jesus Christ give?»

For him Clare and Sylvester were the mouthpieces of God. Masseo answered:

«To Sister Clare and to Fr. Sylvester the Lord has revealed His will: that you go through the world and preach, because He has not chosen you for yourself alone, but also for the salvation of others.»

Francis rose from his knees, and returned to the brothers. With great assurance he then said to his companions:

«Let us go out in the name of God.»

He took his stick and went off into the country in the direction of Montefalco.

BROTHER GILES

The Poor Ladies of St. Damian's were able to get along without the visits of St. Francis, but not without visits from priests, spiritual advisors and someone to hear their confessions.

Through the grille of their simple choir the Ladies heard Mass every morning, and through the bars of the lattice window the mystical recluses received the Bread of the soul, the Host consecrated on the altar by the hands of the priest. Francis saw to it that the worthiest priests and the most prudent confessors were sent to St. Damian's.

Shortly after the death of the Father, the post of spiritual advisor to St. Damian's was taken over by an English brother-priest, a man of the deepest spiritual insight. He was called Alexander of Hales and brought with his cool northern outlook a quiet calm of a truly contemplative soul.

He spoke in a well-ordered tranquil manner with a clear expression and good presentation in whose shining image were reflected the souls of Clare and her companions.

When he preached in the dark little church of St. Damian's, it seemed that from the ceiling darkened by the candle smoke a heavenly light shone and the lilies on the altar gave forth a perfume of paradise.

As companion to Brother Alexander to the convent of the Ladies went Brother Giles, a truly countrified man who, while working in the fields, had heard the call of Francis and brought to the group of first Franciscans the crude, good sense of a man of the soil.

Uninstructed, as much as Alexander of Hales was well educated, crude, as much as Alexander was delicate, it seemed almost as if the two had been particularly chosen to prove how the evangelical ideal could be realized in persons of very diverse natures and educations.

Although the Italian farm-hand could not match the Englishman in study, in one thing they were both equal: in a great fervour of soul that in Alexander showed itself in a delicate and polite language, while in Giles it gushed forth in straight-from-the-shoulder remarks and popular proverbs.

While the English Brother spoke, Giles would sit in a corner of the church, his legs crossed, and his tonsured head resting on his knees. One might have thought he was sleeping, but he was listening and meditating. The honeyed words of Alexander of Hales had a sweetness that filled him with joy.

In spite of this he feared that the Ladies on the other side of the grille were not getting very much consolation at all, so he slowly stood up and interrupted:

«Stop talking, Master, because I want to speak!» With clumsy gestures he shouted out with reference to humility:

«The way to go up, is to go down!»

In his harsh country voice he asked:

«How could we possibly carry on our back a heavy millstone that would keep our head always bent down?»

Then he said:

«When you're in a fight and you want to win, lose; because the way to win is to lose.»

Remembering his former position as a farm-hand, he said:

«This world is a great farm where he who has the largest field has the most work.»

Turning to the Ladies behind the grille, he called:

«Our flesh is a forest where the devil gathers wood.»

Alexander of Hales humbly stopped his sermon in order to listen too and to allow these words of the country Brother.

Sometimes it seemed that Brother Giles exaggerated with his straightforward and solid wisdom, when he said:

«Among all the virtues, I would choose chastity.»

«But is not charity a much greater virtue?». asked the Doctor of Theology tactfully.

The countryman gave the Doctor an artful look, and answered:

«And what thing could ever be more chaste than charity itself?»

Alexander of Hales smiled and nodded his head in agreement with Giles's words.

And the finest lesson that Alexander left behind him with the Poor Ladies of St. Damian's was that of humility in remaining silent at the request of the unlearned brother and to approve his words of simplicity which were inspired by a wisdom that made doctors even of the unlearned.

THE TEARS OF CLARE

When the visits from her spiritual Fathers became less frequent and the little church did not resound with the voice of Francis, Clare then had recourse to the great Master of all masters, the Saviour himself.

She placed herself before the crucifix and meditated deeply on the Five Wounds of Our Blessed Lord. In this she faithfully followed the example of Francis. It seemed as though, in some miraculous way, she already knew that those wounds would be impressed on the body of her earthly master, and that they would become the seal of the Franciscan way of life.

The Passion of Christ was the text in which Clare read and re-read the lessons of holiness. Even when she was working, when she was eating, she had always before her mind the image of the crucified Saviour; she recalled all the pains of this divine Victim, and she quietly and willingly suffered with Him.

Especially in the afternoon between the hours of midday and three o'clock, her participation in the Passion of Christ was acute and sorrowful. It was the time when Jesus died on the Cross. The evening shadows began to spread over the olive trees round St. Damian's, and in the interior of the convent noises had ceased. In the silence of the violet twilight of dusk, Clare felt her soul oppressed with a secret wish to weep upon the lifeless head of the Saviour.

Consequently, she increased her penance, drew to her body the bristly hair shirt that she wore, and gave full play to her devout piety. «Her eyes,» wrote her first biographer, «were like two fountains of water, and all her face and her breast were saturated with tears. She cried unashamedly before the crucifix, considering the death of Jesus.» Her beautiful eyes became red with weeping.

Little by little her tears marked furrows in her cheeks. The tempter, who thought he would find in Clare still some remnant of feminine vanity, took the occasion to taunt her. He appeared to her as a child and said in a sweet voice:

«Why do you cry so much? See how swollen you are, and very soon you will go blind.»

But Clare answered:

«If God is in the soul, one can never go blind.»

She wept even during the night, with her head on her wooden pillow, which was wet as though it had been left out in the rain. Even then the tempter did not leave her alone but came, in the darkness of the dormitory, whispering to her:

«What is the use of these tears? Don't you see that you will destroy your brain because it will soon come out through your nose? You will also mar your beautiful face and eventually lose your mind.»

But Clare answered the insidious voice:

«I lament always over the Passion of my Saviour, and this will not corrupt my mind; if the grace of God, my Creator and my Saviour, helps me in my sorrow, I shall maintain my composure.»

In fact tears acted as a release for her sorrowing soul, strengthened by divine grace. As regards her appearance, her face was beautiful even by natural standards, but this was more and more enhanced by the serene composure of supernatural beauty.

Clare mourned, indeed, but between her tears there shone the power of a soul in love with Christ, just as in springtime the sun shines between the showers.

However, contrary to the expectation of the devil, instead of crying more on account of the pain suffered, Clare smiled with joy. She was happy to bear even material abuse and to suffer physical pain inflicted upon her body by the enemy of her soul.

Seeing that no good came of his insidious temptations, the Evil One had recourse to physical violence. On one occasion when Clare was meditating on the sufferings of the Redeemer, she received a most severe clout across the head. Her tears were not then only those of piety, but also of bodily pain.

THE CANTICLE OF
THE CREATURES

C lare prayed and mourned before the crucifix. Francis himself became a living crucifix. Towards the end of the summer of 1224, Francis had received the Stigmata, the five wounds of Our Lord impressed on his own body, on Mount Alverna where he had gone to pray and meditate among the cleft rocks and the towering trees. On his hands and feet and side these bleeding wounds of the Saviour appeared.

Wounded in this way, he came down from the mountain slowly and painfully, seated on an ass, in the general direction of Assisi:

«Good-bye, thou Mount of God, good-bye Mount Alverna, holy mountain! May God the Father, God the Son and God the Holy Spirit bless thee!»

He said these words from the top of Mount Casella, turning towards Alverna, but he could no longer see it, because his sight was clouded. What the tempter had foretold to Clare was verified in Francis; his eyes were burning and painful and he was nearly blind.

By the time he arrived at Foligno he was very ill, indeed, almost dying, and at Rieti he found that the Papal court was in residence there, and some doctors were called to him. One of them thought to cure him by cauterizing his temples with a red hot instrument. Francis allowed himself to be thus tormented without saying anything, except a remark to the fire itself:

«Deal gently with me, Brother Fire, for I have always had thee in high regard for the sake of the Lord.»

But this sort of cure brought him no relief. The body, which he called Brother Ass, was one mass of pain. His eyes gave him great pain because it seemed as if there were splinters of glass scraping on the pupils; his chest pained because of the wound in his side; his stomach was ulcerated by fastings and the spleen destroyed by fatigue; his wounded hands, his swollen legs and the gaping wounds from the insteps through to the soles of his feet were all painful.

In the summer of 1225 Francis, in this condition, wished to stay a while at St. Damian's. Now that he had become similar to the Crucified, he would be able to stay among the Poor Ladies without any misgivings.

He was now able to say of himself: «Behold the man!» And Clare met him, exhausted, emaciated, wounded, groping about in the brightness of the sun as though he were in darkness.

It was not allowed that Francis be accommodated in the convent of the Poor Ladies, so Clare had a little hut of reeds built for him in the garden. For a bed Francis wanted nothing but straw. There among the olive trees at St. Damian's, surrounded by the shrill sound of the cicala, he was looked after by Clare and her companions, who were glad to have Francis among them, though they were sad at his condition. The 'living crucifix' that he was was a constant anxiety to them.

Francis smiled on them and received their loving ministrations. He did not let them know during the day what torment he had to go through during the night. When, in obedience to the Rule, the doors of the convent had been closed, Francis remained outside in his little hut, quite unable to sleep. Starving mice came out from under the straw to bite the toes of his feet. Restless and in pain, he turned from side to side, but could get no peace.

However, instead of bewailing all this and becoming morose over it, he felt his soul was full of great happiness. Every pang was turned into a joy because he realised that they came from the Saviour who had suffered to redeem us all. Everything was grand and good because they were the works of the Lord, and even sorrow and infirmity were only good things if accepted in the Name of Jesus and His Passion. To suffer with Jesus was to suffer with God, and this was the great privilege that gave Francis such exuberant joy.

One morning after a night more disturbed than usual, while the dawn glittered among the silvery foliage of the olive trees at St. Damian's, Francis met Clare at the door of his hut. The morning mist still swirled about the olive trees around St. Damian's, and there he recited to her a new canticle in praise of all God's creatures:

Most High, Omnipotent, Good Lord.
>   *Thine be the praise, the glory, the honour, and*
>   *benediction.*
>   *To Thee alone, Most High, they are due,*
>   *And no man is worthy to mention Thee.*

Be Thou praised, my Lord, with all Thy creatures,
>   *above all Brother Sun,*
>   *Who gives the day, and lightens us therewith.*
>   *And he is beautiful and radiant with great splen-*
>   *dour,*
>   *Of Thee, Most High, he bears similitude.*

*Be Thou praised, my Lord, of Sister Moon and the
Stars,*
*In the heavens Thou hast formed them, clear and
precious and comely.*

Be Thou praised, my Lord, of Brother Wind,
*And of the air and the cloud, and of fair and of
all weather,*
*By which Thou givest to Thy creatures suste-
nance.*

Be Thou praised, my Lord, of Sister Water,
*Which is much useful and humble, precious and
pure.*

Be Thou praised, my Lord, of Brother Fire,
By which Thou hast lightened the night,
And he is beautiful and joyful, robust and strong.

Be Thou praised, my Lord, of our Sister Mother Earth,
Which sustains and hath us in rule,
*And produces divers fruits with coloured flowers
and herbs.*

Clare listened with rapture, and then joined
with Francis in this great praise of God and His
creatures. Perhaps she also felt that she was as

precious as the stars and as humble and pure as the water. The joy of her soul knew no bounds on that morning of great splendour when Francis, in a voice broken with sobs, sang:

Be Thou praised, my Lord, of those who pardon for
*   Thy love,*
*   And endure sickness and tribulations.*
*   Blessed are they who will endure it in peace,*
*   For by Thee, Most High, they shall be crowned.*

This was the great lesson that Clare received and which she preserved with perfect fidelity: to forgive for the love of Jesus, and to bear infirmity and tribulations in peace and joy.

The last verse of the Canticle Francis offered to all his followers, but to none more particularly than Clare:

Praise and bless my Lord, and give Him thanks,
*   And serve Him with great humility.*

The convent of St. Damian was awake. In that little corner of Paradise the Poor Ladies of Clare would always serve the Lord in happiness and great humility.

THE LAST MEETING

Even sick and blind Francis could not stay settled. He therefore left St. Damian's on his own, and to one who wanted to go with him he said:

«See, there goes a blind man, who has no other guide but a dog; I have no wish to be better than he.»

The sick man walked with great difficulty, and kept muttering to his tired body:

«Cheer up, Brother Ass, and forgive me; just a little while yet and you may rest for good.»

Instinctively he took the road to Assisi, for he was returning to die in his own town. There he was the guest of the Bishop, and though so near to dying Francis was still singing.

Later, however, when he felt that Sister Death was very near indeed, he requested that he be taken down to the Portiuncula; he wanted to die at St. Mary of the Angels. His companions arranged him as comfortably as possible on a barrow, and thus they took him from the town. When he was half way there, he asked them to put the litter down on the ground, and there, turning towards Assisi, he gave it a final blessing.

When Clare learned that Francis had returned to the Portiuncula to die there, she longed to visit him and to assist at his last agony. The convent of St. Damian seemed now a veritable prison! She would have loved to have opened the door and run towards the woods at St. Mary of the Angels, as she had done so long ago when she fled from her home.

But Francis would in no way allow it; he would not permit her to leave the convent. Yet, knowing the sorrow of Clare and the Poor Ladies, he told a brother to go and visit them:

«Go and tell Sister Clare that she must put aside all sorrow and sadness on account of not seeing me. They will see me after my death, and that will console them a little.»

On the other hand, he then asked that another lady should come to him at the Portiuncula, a Roman widow named Jacopa dei Settesoli. Clare and Jacopa were to Francis what Martha and Mary were to Our Blessed Lord. Clare was the woman of prayer and contemplation; Jacopa the woman of action and assistance. From her he received gifts of cloth, of candles, and even of a certain marzipan sweet made with flour and honey. Francis considered her almost a man: while he always spoke of Clare as Sister Clare, he referred to Jacopa as Brother Jacopa.

Before entering into his agony, Francis asked that his frock be removed and that he be placed naked upon the bare earth. But the Guardian of the Portiuncula requested that he put some clothes on and handed him a wrap. Francis took this tunic but made it known that he wished to die possessed of nothing, and in this way, stretched on the ground, he renewed his espousals to Lady Poverty.

At sunset on the third of October he expired. At the moment of his passing his death cell at the Portiuncula was surrounded by a swarm of trilling skylarks. Francis had always loved these little creatures because they seemed to him images of his own friars. Dressed in plain grey, without any ornaments, they lived on the earth, but hardly was the sun up each day that they took to their wings with great joy. His brothers, too, clad in homespun grey material, were to live in poverty in the world, but always with great joy in recognition of the Lord, the Sun of the soul.

Brother Jacopa laid out the body of Francis and placed an embroidered kerchief over his face: Clare cried and prayed the whole night through in the rough choir stalls at St. Damian's.

The next day the people and the clergy came down from Assisi, and the people from all the neighbouring towns and villages came flocking to Our Lady of the Angels. The glorification of the little Poor Man had begun. His body was taken from the Portiuncula immediately to the town. Instead of going by the direct road, down which he had been carried a few days before, the funeral cortege took a longer route in order to pass by St. Damian's.

Francis had promised Clare that she would see him again: now returning to her he was followed by priests with burning torches and by people waving palms which they broke off trees on the way.

At St. Damian's the Poor Ladies were waiting behind the grille. Clare, her eyes burning with tears, waited at the door of the church. From far off came the chanting of those who accompanied the body. Then silence. Eventually the hearse arrived in front of St. Damian's, and they brought the stretcher bearing the body into the church.

See there, the wounded feet! Those wounded hands! Behold the wound in his side, and his waxen face composed in the solemn peace of death!

From the other side of the grille the Poor

Ladies were sorrowfully sobbing. The door of the grille slowly opened: it was the last meeting on earth of Clare and her «living crucifix.» She was no longer weeping. Palid under her black veil, she came forward and kissed the wounds of his feet, of his hands, and in his side. She gradually backed away as the other Ladies came out and did the same.

When she rose from her silent sorrow, the church was empty. Faintly in the distance one could hear the trampling feet of the mourners as the funeral procession slowly went up towards the town.

But St. Damian's was not forsaken. Jesus Crucified was still there. Francis, indeed, was dead, but his Master and suffering Saviour was still there on the cross always and for all men.

THE DEFENCE OF POVERTY

The Pope had come to Assisi. He had come to proclaim to the entire Christian world that Francis, the son of Pietro Bernardone, was a Saint.

It was 1228. Only two years had passed since the perfect Poor Man died, lying on the bare ground at the Portiuncula. These two years alone had sufficed to open and close the process of his canonization, for the Church did not need much time to establish in her infallible manner the holiness of Francis.

Time was not needed for the people. They immediately held him in veneration as they carried his body — Brother Ass — up to the town and into the little church of St. George. On that body already existed the seals of holiness, impressed by Jesus, those Five Wounds known as the Stigmata on his hands and feet and side.

Pope Gregory IX had purposely arrived in Assisi to add the weight of his authority to those miraculous signs, and to raise this Poor Man, God's jester, barefooted, macerated and wounded, to the glories of the altar.

Gregory had been Pope for only one year; previously he was Cardinal Hugolino of the Orsini family. As Cardinal he had known Francis and had helped him to compose and get the approval for his Rule of Life. Therefore, he knew

all about Francis and about Clare and the Poor
Ladies as well.

The Pope wanted to visit St. Damian's and
see for himself what were the practical effects
of their Rule of Poverty, concerning which he
had had long discussions with Francis.

At Rome the demands of Francis and Clare
had seemed just a little too bold. While many
other people asked for privileges and favours,
Francis and Clare asked simply to be allowed
to live in poverty.

When this request of Clare asking for herself and the Poor Ladies the privilege of possess-
ing nothing and of begging had been placed before
Pope Innocent III, the Pope remarked:

«Never has such a privilege — to live in
such poverty — been requested of the Holy See!»

And now another Pope, Gregory IX, rode
out from the gate of Assisi, down through the
olive groves, to visit and see for himself just
how it was possible to live in that way. He took
the short road and quickly came down to the
small convent with its roughly built walls, followed by Cardinals, prelates and knights. The
Holy Father knocked at the door of the convent
encircled by pargetless walls.

The exclusiveness of the cloister can be dispensed with by the Pope, so he went right inside to meet the Poor Ladies, who knelt before him.

Clare was his guide:

«See, here is the little church that Francis repaired with his own hands. This is the choir with its grille, opened so that the Poor Ladies might be able to kiss the wounds of the Saint. This is the cloister garden with its well. This the dormitory. This the sick room.» Finally, the garden, so large as a tiny piece of delicate embroidery.

Gregory IX looked round him, and was turning everything over in his mind: the choir stalls of rough wood, the large refectory table, the mattresses of twigs and wooden pillows. He noticed the Sisters' clean attire, but full of mended pieces and patches, their bare feet, their work-worn hands. He measured the garden where nothing grew except two rosemary shrubs and some small sages.

How was anyone able to live in this state of poverty? How did the Poor Ladies get their sustenance? All monasteries and convents always possessed fields and farms from which they were able to provide their necessities of life.

On the contrary at St. Damian's within the cloister walls, the Poor Ladies had no possessions. How could they live?

«On alms, Holy Father,» replied Clare.

«But if hard times come, wars, famines, how would you manage then?»

«Divine Providence, Holy Father.»

«Your Rule is far too strict. Holy Mother Church cannot allow her chosen daughters to be thus exposed to need without any defence.»

«Our defence is Christ crucified, and His Vicar on earth.»

Gregory looked straight into the firm features of Clare and appeared to be searching into her innermost thoughts. He spoke to her slowly to give this strong willed woman time to reflect.

«My daughter, if you fear the vow of Holy Poverty which you have already made, I may dispense you from it. You know that Jesus gave His Vicar power to bind and to loose as well, and that which is bound on earth is bound also in heaven.»

Cardinals and prelates nodded assent. They found the words of the Pope very wise. It was a good thing to mitigate the severity of this Rule. The knights and the rest of the entourage agreed completely: the sight of such extreme poverty had disturbed them. Certainly it was necessary to alleviate the harshness of the life of these ladies!

Clare became pale at these words of the Holy Father, as if she were being threatened. Her eyes filled with tears as though she had been punished for something. She fell on her knees before the Pope and, in a voice choking with emotion, appealed to him:

«Holy Father, I am not afraid of the vow I have taken. I know quite well that you are able to release and to absolve me from the vow I have made.»

There was a pause, and then she continued in a stronger voice:

«Holy Father, absolve me, indeed, from my sins, release me from my faults, but not — not from the privilege of holy poverty, from which I have no wish to ever be released!»

And all the Poor Ladies, faithful to the teaching of St. Francis, were in agreement with Clare. From Christ's Vicar they asked an absolution from their sins, but also a strengthening of their vow of poverty.

CROSS BUNS

Gregory IX spent quite some time at Assisi; but before leaving the district, he wanted once again to return to St. Damian's.

Now officially the Church recognized the heroic virtues of the Poor Man of Assisi. The little town was crowded with friars who came from far and near for the canonization: the son of Pietro di Bernardone was a Saint with the halo of glory shining round him. The fame of St. Francis reflected throughout the entire Church, so that in whichever country his friars went, they were given a ready welcome, and within a few years the Order of Friars Minor — commonly called «Franciscans» — became greatly esteemed in many parts of the world.

Thus there were very many, indeed, who followed the Rule of St. Francis. But above all and better than all there was Clare, who remained completely faithful to the teaching of the Saint, maintaining a perfect poverty.

Pope Gregory IX thought many times over the answer Clare had given him when he visited St. Damian's: «Holy Father, absolve me from my sins, but not from my vow of poverty.» He could see that she understood plainly the spirit of St. Francis and intended to follow it to the letter. With this in mind, the Pope felt he could not leave Assisi without going once again down through the olive groves to the small convent where he had breathed the pure air of Franciscanism.

Having heard this time that he was coming, Clare and her sisters decorated the church with flowers, polished the tables with oil, and scattered palm and olive leaves along the roadway just outside of the convent. Although poor, she wanted to do her very best to honour the Vicar of Christ. Her poverty was not to be a proud poverty, for a proud and condescending poverty is like mouldy bread: it is poisonous and nourishes no one.

When the Pope arrived, he blessed the Poor Ladies of St. Damian's and spoke to them as a father to daughters. Clare listened to him with rapt attention. No matter how far advanced she was in holiness and devotion, every word of the Pope was to her a priceless gift. He was Jesus on earth: this was what St. Francis, always loyal to the holy Church, had thought. And she, being a true daughter of his, now addressed the Pope as 'Holy Father.'

On his part, Gregory wished to hear Clare speak as well. He listened with admiration as she discoursed of heavenly and divine things. So the time passed quicker than they thought and the noon hour had already struck. Clare became suddenly aware of the fact that the Pontiff would not be able to get back to the town for his midday meal.

This was completely unexpected and she was a bit confused: but willing as ever, she had the table prepared immediately. There was nothing but bread, stale bread received as alms. Clare had the rolls of bread laid on the table, then knelt down before the Pope and asked him to bless the bread. Instead, he said to her:

«Dear, faithful Clare, I want you to bless this bread yourself; make over it the Sign of Christ's Cross.»

«Forgive me, Holy Father,» said Clare, «in this I would be greatly to be blamed, if I, a worthless woman, presumed to give a blessing in this way in the presence of Christ's Vicar.»

The Pope answered:

«Well then, in order that it be not set down to presumption, and indeed, that further merit may be yours, I command you by Holy Obedience to bless these loaves by making the Sign of the Cross with your hand.»

Clare would not refuse an order from the Holy Father, so she rose to her feet, and raising her right hand in the air, made a large Sign of the Cross, calling on the name of the Father and of the Son and of the Holy Spirit.

As she finished the words, the Pope and his cardinals and the prelates of his entourage and the Poor Ladies as well who were standing round the table, saw, quite suddenly, as if by a miracle, that a large cross appeared on every piece of bread: a cross incised into the hard crust of the loaves!

THE BREAD OF ANGELS

Bread flavoured with a little oil was most often the only food the Poor Ladies had. At times they might not even have had that if Clare had not worked a miracle.

What they never lacked was the Eucharistic Bread, the Bread of Angels. Clare could manage without the ordinary bread, but she could do nothing at all unless she received that Bread which the priest consecrated on the altar and distributed to her and her sisters at the grille.

In this Clare showed herself a true follower of Francis who never tired of saying and writing to his brothers:

«Brothers, I pray all of you, kissing your feet and with as great devotion as I am able, to show the greatest reverence and every honour that you are able, to the holy Body and Blood of Our Saviour, Jesus Christ.»

He had told them on another occasion:

«If I should happen to meet at the same time a saint come down from heaven and a poor priest, I should first of all honour the priest, running to kiss his hands. I would say to the saint: 'Wait a minute, St. Laurence, because this man's hands have touched the Word who is Life and possess a divine power.'»

And what, indeed, is that divine power of the priest? Precisely that he is able to change a piece of bread into the Body of Jesus and administer the Eucharist to the faithful. Clare had a great devotion to the Eucharist and a great reverence for the priest, to whom Christ at the Last Supper gave the power of consecrating bread and wine.

Whenever she was ill, she was accustomed to sit up in bed of twigs or straw with a small sack supporting her shoulders from behind, and ask for flax which she spun, wove, and sewed into corporals and finger cloths. She then sent these as gifts to poor priests, because she realized that the altar linens should be new and clean, especially those smaller pieces that actually touch the chalice.

It happened one year that she was in the sad position of not being able to receive Holy Communion on Christmas Night. To leave out Holy Communion was a great sorrow to Clare, especially on feast days. The Nativity was for her, as it was for Francis, the most moving feast of the whole year, because on that day God, the Creator of the universe, was born in a stable, a poor infant among the poorest of men.

«If I could speak to the Emperor,» St. Francis had said one day, «I would ask him to give a general command that all those who were able should scatter corn and grain along the streets on Christmas Day, so that on that most solemn of all feasts the little birds might have plenty of food.»

And indeed, just as eager as those little birds were to peck at the grains of corn, so was Clare eager on that Christmas Night to get to the chapel in order to receive the Blessed Sacrament, the Food of the Soul.

However, that year she was gravely ill and confined to bed. That others should stay with her, was not her wish at all, for she wanted all of them to be in the chapel for the Midnight Mass and to receive the Bread of Angels. She remained on her sick bed, alone in the bare and poor dormitory, lying upon her uncomfortable bed with arms crossed over her bosom, longing ardently to be in the chapel with the rest for the sacred functions on that holy night.

She could hear the bells ringing out over the snow, calling the people to the great Sacrifice of the Mass. With her heart overflowing with love for the Holy Child, the bells seemed to her sweeter and more full of meaning in their steady and joyous pealing.

Fondly she thought of the night when St. Francis had made a live crib in the woods of Greccio, a true scene of the Nativity. Her meditation became a deep act of love towards the merciful God who came into this world to suffer and to save man from sin. With the angels she repeated their hymn full of great joy and hope:

«Glory be to God on high, and on earth peace to men who are God's friends.»

Thus the time went by. The bells ceased. After a while Clare heard the light footsteps of the sisters and saw the flicker of the lamp, as they returned to the cold dormitory in the early hours of the morning.

«O Mother Clare,» they said, «what a great joy and consolation we have had on this holy night. Would that it had pleased God for you to have been with us!»

From her straw bed Clare smiled, and said to them:

«My dear sisters, thanks and praise to my dear Saviour, Christ, because this night I have had an even greater consolation than you. Through the intercession of our holy Father, St. Francis, I assisted at that very same solemnity on this Christmas Eve. With my own ears I heard the singing, and I was present at the entire Mass. I saw the Holy Mother and St. Joseph, and was present at the birth of the Child Jesus in the manger of Bethlehem.

«But that, indeed, was not all. I have received a most extraordinary grace, because Our Blessed Lord satisfied my most burning desire and He Himself brought me Holy Communion. May He be forever blessed for His great goodness to His poor, sick servant, whom He wished to nourish with spiritual food.»

THE SARACENS OF
FREDERICK II

Assisi was not only the cradle of Franciscan poverty; it was also the proud centre of the Ghibeline Party.

It is said, with how much truth it is hard to tell, that at the old granite font in the old Cathedral, after Francis the son of Pietro di Bernardone, there was baptized another child Frederick, who was the son of Henry and a nephew of the Emperor Barbarossa. This young German princeling must have been resident at that time at La Rocca, the Castle of Assisi, under the Pope's protection.

A fact it is that the Pope had shown a great tenderness towards this young prince of the Swabian dynasty. He saw that he was well instructed, reared him with great care, protected him from his enemies, and finally he had even succeeded in helping him into court life and coronation at the age of eighteen.

But by then the young king, full of ambition, showed very little gratitude or reverence for the Holy Father. Indeed, he turned against the Church, became a schismatic, a heretic, and an infidel.

Frederick was a very intelligent man, a literary person of some pretentions, and a composer of love poems. His admirers referred to him as «The Great Cleric.» He was as courageous and valorous as he was ambitious and self-opinionated, which made his enemies call him «The Hammer of the World.»

Of German stock, he had nevertheless fallen in love with Italy and dreamt of a grand kingdom of sunlit lands in the southern half of the peninsula, stretching from Apulia to Sicily, a strong Ghibeline power, a country in which his will would be law and his pleasure inviolable.

An army of 20,000 Saracens, men of war, disciplined and cruel, was ready at this command. Unfaithful to the true God, they were most faithful to the Emperor, and united the cruel coldness of the north with the bloodlusty ferocity of the south: white teeth, blue eyes, swarthy complexions, sparse beards, tall in stature and nimble in movement, there were no mercenaries more feared than these Saracens whom Frederick II spearheaded in a drive from Sicily towards Rome and beyond.

When about 1240 the news reached Assisi that Frederick the Second's Saracens were advancing through the valley of Spoleto, the town was seized by a paroxysm of fear. Word was sent round the district, and when all from the countryside were gathered within the walls, the great gates of the town were slammed shut securely. From the castle scouts kept watch, gazing out all over the valley to the hills beyond.

Only Clare's «Poor Ladies» remained outside, at St. Damian's without any defence. Before attacking the town these enemy soldiers would have to pass by the poor convent hidden in the olive groves, and they would come without any considerations of respect for the holy spot or its devoted inhabitants. What considerations of mercy could be expected from these infidel Saracens, hirelings of a schismatic sovereign?

On the hill of Subasio, the town, enclosed by its limestone walls, seemed more pale than ever. In the depopulated countryside the olive trees seemed more ashen-grey than usual.

Terror of Frederick's Saracens spread everywhere. The fear in the hearts of the people was increased by the stillness on the landscape: along the horizon great billows of smoke went up from innumerable fires, and terrifying news came of pillage, slaughter, and destruction.

Meanwhile the Poor Ladies at St. Damian's prayed and fasted. When the news came that the army had arrived, Clare was stretched on her rough mattress very ill. The glint of helmets and the tips of barbaric pikes could be seen moving about through the pallid green foliage of the olive trees. Swarthy faces with cold steel eyes and thick lips were already peering over the surrounding walls.

In due time heavy banging was heard at the convent door; and Clare, raising herself a little, asked what it was all about. They told her in hushed and terrified voices that it was Frederick's Saracens.

Clare got up with great effort and told them to bring her the silver and ivory monstrance in which the Sacred Hosts were kept. Taking this, she then went with it in her hands to the large window opening onto the square, and raising it she showed Jesus in the Blessed Sacrament to this infidel soldiery of an anti-Christian army.

While she did this she prayed:

«I ask Thee, O my Lord, that it might please Thee not to let these poor servants of Thine fall into the hands of cruel infidels and pagans.»

And then she added another petition:

«I ask Thee, O My Lord, that Thou wouldst also watch over this town and all those good people, who, for the love of Thee, help us and provide our necessities.»

From the silver and ivory monstrance it seemed that a voice came forth as sweet as that of a child:

«Because of your love, I will watch over you and them always.»

A little time passed, and then the Saracens' faces began to disappear from around the convent grounds. They could see the shining helmets and the glint of lances moving away through the olive groves.

The scouts at Assisi were watching from far off and expecting the assault of the Saracens under their walls. But no shouts of war disturbed that night. When morning came the gates were able to be thrown open, and the people came and went and even stopped once again in peace.

Certainly, at the power of Clare's prayer, a Hand from high had made the army captains change their plans. Frederick's hordes were switched away by another route, far from the convent of St. Damian and the town of Assisi.

INFIRMITY AND SUFFERING

I t would seem that just before he died, Francis was thinking of Clare when, in the little garden at St. Damian's, he sang:

Be Thou praised, O my Lord,
For those who pardon for thy love,
And put up with every infirmity and tribulation.

Clare was actually in sickness for twenty-eight years, from the age of thirty-two to sixty. From time to time her sisters at St. Damian's were afraid of losing her, but each time she reassured them:

«My daughters, God does not wish that I die yet, but that I remain with you in this miserable body.»

Her mattress became her throne, from which she spoke, especially to the young, of resignation and patience.

Over the years St. Damian's had become an irresistible magnet to many souls. A writer of the times has left on record:

«The young girls who run to Clare are more numerous than the bees that rest on flowers in the springtime.»

As we have seen, Pacifica di Guelfuccio was her first companion, then her sister Agnes, then Benvenuta da Perugia. Next came Balvina,

Cecilia, Philippa, Amata, Christina, Angeluccia, Lucia, Beatrice, Benedetta, Illuminata, Anastasia, Giacomina, Mansueta, Benvenuta, Benricevuta, Bennata, Consolata, Chiarella, Pacifica, Vertera, Massariola, and finally her own mother, Ortolana, and a great many others.

From her sickbed Clare radiated an influence of love that drew to her girls and ladies, not only from Assisi and its district but from the farthest countries. An historian of that period could say:

«There was hardly a kingdom in the world, or a baron's estate, where there was not built a convent under the Rule and teaching of St. Clare.»

For the love of poverty the blond princess Agnes, daughter of the King of Bohemia, she who had been engaged to Frederick II, cut away her hair and girded herself with the cord of St. Francis. Clare wrote to her:

«You poor virgin, come closer to the poor Christ.»

Agnes answered:

«Blessed thou art, poverty, for thou bringest eternal riches to those who embrace thee.»

A little later it was the turn of a queen,

Elizabeth of Hungary, who joined the Third Order of St. Francis, and she was followed by others like Ermentrude of Cologne, who became a Poor Clare.

Poverty, however, would not have been much use on its own, if it were not supported in illness, and Clare gave them this example of patiently tolerating infirmity and tribulation. She prayed without ceasing and without stopping she worked, unless on those occasions when it happened that her soul was rapt in contemplation.

To one of her disciples who rendered filial assistance, she said:

«When you notice that I am not aware of things around me, you may come but do not call to me unless to you I seem to be in imminent danger of death.»

Especially on Fridays she was filled with sorrow and went into ecstasies while meditating on the Passion of Our Lord. On one occasion she remained out of herself for a whole day. When night came the sister in attendance on her came towards her with a lighted candle.

«Why this light?» asked the sick Clare. «It is still morning.»

«My dear Mother,» answered the infirmarian, «you have already gone through the whole of Friday and we are now in the night of Saturday. You have slept almost twenty-four hours.»

Clare looked around her and said with a sigh:

«Blessed be this sleep, my daughter.»

This experience was not sleep, and during her ecstasies the things she saw and heard were not dreams.

It was in this way that she became convinced that she would not die until she had seen the Pope again. He was at that time in France. However, not long afterwards Pope Innocent IV returned to Genoa, proceeding thence to Milan and on to Bologna, and eventually arriving at Perugia in November, 1253.

When he had heard that Clare lay seriously ill, he first sent along the Cardinal of Ostia, and then he himself arrived at Assisi and hurried down to St. Damian's. Coming to her bedside he proffered her his hand to kiss. To Clare to kiss the Holy Father's hand seemed too privileged a gesture:

«No, my Lord,» she said, «you are the Vicar of Christ and the successor of the Apostle Peter. It is not your hand that I should kiss, but your feet!»

Noting her greater reverence, the Pope ordered a stool to be brought, so that he might sit in such a position that Clare would be able to kiss his foot. The sick nun performed this act of humble devotion with tears of joy, by kissing both the insteps and soles of the Holy Father's feet. And then she asked the Pope for absolution from her sins:

«I have a great need of it,» she said humbly.

«Would to God that I had just as much need of it,» remarked the Pope, feeling before such deep humility a sense of remorse at his own exalted position.

THE PAPAL BULL

Every time Clare met the Pope, she asked for two things: the forgiveness of her sins and the approbation of her vow of poverty.

The Abbess of St. Damian's particularly wanted a Papal Bull, that is, an official letter written on sheepskin, having attached to it the leaden pontifical seal, impressed on the one side with the coat of arms of the reigning Pope and on the other, the figures of Sts. Peter and Paul.

The Bull that Clare wanted, and had asked for, would have to contain the approval of the Rule that she had followed at St. Damian's under the guidance of St. Francis: the Rule which imposed a perfect and very strict poverty without any exception or mitigation.

For seventeen days Clare had eaten nothing, and her body was reduced to a skeleton, with her eyes, however, burning brightly in expectation of this final great grace. The Papal Court was at Assisi, and every day Cardinals and bishops in twos and threes came down to St. Damian's to see and to speak with this chosen daughter of St. Francis. Clare received them all with a charming smile in spite of her pain, watching intently in case they might be bringing the longed-for Bull. Not seeing it, she would then turn her head slowly aside, close her eyes, and murmur a prayer to the Vicar of Christ:

«Do come and help me.»

Before she was called from this life, she wanted to have this Papal Bull to leave to her sisters as a legacy, so that after her death no one might be tempted to assail the strong wall of poverty with the weapons of human compassion.

She had, indeed, been very adamant in repulsing all attacks on her Rule. She had refused privileges and rejected concessions; her absolute fidelity to St. Francis had remained invincible. While ever she was in charge, even from her deathbed of twigs and straw, ill and weak, no assault of compassionate allurement had frightened her. She consistantly refused to look on poverty as a peril or a weakness. On the contrary, very strict poverty was for her, as it had been for Francis, an invincible weapon and an irresistible power for holiness.

However, now that on deathbed she felt the approach of Sister Death, now that she was about to relinquish the post of command and of battle, she wanted to leave her sisters another weapon which would be nothing less than a reflexion of her own unbending will.

She wished that the Vicar of Christ would accept this will of hers; she requested from the

Church an official document in which the Rule in all its integrity would be approved. Consequently, she waited for a Papal Bull.

For this reason she gazed lovingly at the hands of the Cardinals and Bishops who came to visit her; then, not seeing this roll of parchment with the leaden bull, the seal hanging from it, she would sigh again, turn her head away, close her eyes and repeat her silent prayer.

In those days she had visits also from the remaining companions of St. Francis, now old men. Brother Leo, «The Little Sheep of God»; Brother Angelo, «The Warrior of Christ»; and Brother Giles, «The Knight of the Round Table.» And Clare would ask them:

«Have you at hand anything new from sweet Jesus?»

She meant the strength of words newly afire with love for Jesus, words such as the deep mysticism of these men, the old followers of Francis, was able to give her. She asked that they pray for her, these old and time-worn men from the woods around St. Mary of the Angels. Pray that she would not die before that Papal Bull arrived at St. Damian's!

Then at last came the Pontifical document,

only one day after it had been signed by the Pope. It was August 10th, 1253. Accurately rolled, with the seal intact, it was brought to the bed of the dying nun. She kissed the seal on both sides and asked them to unroll the document and read it to her. She then closed her eyes, the better to follow the words.

The Bull said:

Innocent, Bishop, Servant of the Servants of God, to his daughters in Jesus Christ, Clare, Abbess, and to the other Ladies of the Convent of St. Damian at Assisi, health and Apostolic Blessing. You have humbly asked Us to sanction with Our Apostolic authority the form of life which St. Francis gave you, and which you have embraced of your own free will, therefore obliging yourselves to a common life in spiritual unity with the vow of most high poverty. Wherefore, attending to the desires of your piety, We very willingly fully ratify your Rule and strengthen it with Our Apostolic Authority...

Clare reopened her eyes and tears of joy were on her face. She seemed in ecstasy as the reader continued:

...There is no permission given to anyone whatsoever to infringe this Act of Our Authority, or to be

so bold as to act against it, indeed, should anyone dare attempt this, let him know that he will immediately incur the anger of Almighty God and of his Apostles, Peter and Paul...

She stretched out her hands and looked intently at the leaden seal having the impressions of St. Peter with his keys and St. Paul with his sword. From now on there existed a sure defence of the way of life at St. Damian's and its privilege of holy poverty.

Clare then read the date:

Given at Assisi, the ninth day of the month of August in the eleventh year of our Pontificate.

She drew the parchment to herself and closed her hands over it in the form of a cross.

The hour of her death was very near.

THE RETINUE OF VIRGINS

With the Bull about holy poverty clasped to her breast, Clare was now ready to die. She was prepared to chant her *Nunc dimittis*: «*Now Thou dost dismiss Thy servant, Lord, in peace,*» since the Pope had ratified and sanctioned her Rule of the poor life.

On the bed where she had been lying through a very long illness, she murmured to her own soul which she felt about to leave the body, now a mere skeleton with fasting and suffering:

«Go forth joyfully in peace to Him who made you, sanctified you, who has always loved and watched over you; go forth to Him who has guided you.»

One of the Poor Ladies standing near hearing these words asked her apprehensively:

«What did you say, holy Mother? To whom were you speaking?»

«I was speaking to my own happy soul,» answered Clare.

A little time later she was again heard to say:

«Blessed art Thou, O my Lord, who hast created me and with Thy Precious Blood hast redeemed me to give me eternal life, which is, indeed, Thyself.»

Smiling she turned to the sister who was in attendance and asked:

«Do you see the King of Glory as I see Him?»

The Poor Ladies of St. Damian's had by now all come together and were kneeling and weeping with sorrow round the bed of their Mother.

Clare had received the Papal Bull only the day before, on August 10th, the feast of St. Laurence. All the course of that night it seemed that even the pitch-dark sky wept, shedding a meteoric shower of tears.

Then came the dawn of a new day and every vestige of sorrow was cast aside. Through the large windows looking out over the countryside, the morning light came in with more than usual brilliance, and Clare's eyes responded to its brightness. However, it was certainly not an ordinary, natural light that came in through the door. Clare turned herself in its direction, and all her sisters likewise turned, more enraptured than stupified.

Afterwards into the little room floated a procession of white-clad virgins, each wearing a golden crown. In their midst came the Virgin of Virgins, more glorious and lovely than all the others. The crown She wore was of such resplendent beauty that it outshone the sun in all its brightness.

The Queen of Virgins came forward ahead of the rest and went towards Clare's bed. She stooped over the dying nun and sweetly embraced her. And while She held Clare in the loving embrace, the Virgin Queen of Heaven motioned to the others to bring forth the tunic of pure gold set with precious stones, and in this the Blessed Virgin enveloped Clare's soul.

On the bed linens there was left only a poor, lifeless corpse.

Accompanied by this retinue of Virgins the happy and glorious soul of Clare went off to Paradise and everlasting joy.

* * *

As that day wore on the news that Clare was dead spread everywhere. From the countryside and from the town, people came running to St. Damian's, all of them with one prayer on their lips:

«St. Clare, pray to God for us!»

The Pope and his court also came for the funeral rites, and the Holy Father ordered that instead of the usual Office of the Dead they should chant the Office of the Virgins.

It seems that the Cardinal of Ostia had retarded the impetus of the Pope and had proposed the normal procedures in expectation of the process of beatification. The Pope accepted this suggestion, and instructed him to deliver the panegyric in honour of St. Clare, already called so by the acclamation of the people.

From Assisi came nobles, soldiers and horsemen. Day and night the little convent was surrounded by armed men, a guard for the holy remains.

St. Francis' body had been left only a very little while at the Portiuncula, for after his death his companions took his body in haste round by St. Damian's and up through the Porta Nuova into the town, where they laid it to rest temporarily in the little church of St. George.

It was not wise to leave so precious a relic in an undefended place outside the walls of the town. The Perugians might come and by force of arms take away the body, because in those times a saint's body was esteemed more than a treasure. Two years afterwards the body of St. Francis was taken from St. George's and buried in the rock under the great new basilica with bastions and walls like a fortress, that was built on the edge of the town by command of Brother Elias.

The townspeople had the same fears for the body of St. Clare. St. Damian's was situated in the open country, protected only by its garden wall. It was for this reason that it was now guarded by armed men, and the nobles of Assisi had mounted a strong guard lest their treasure be taken away from them.

Thereafter it was necessary to arrange for the body to be brought within the town walls. The little church of St. George was free again; and where the Father had rested, it seemed most fitting that the daughter should rest too. So, as in life Clare had imitated the way of St. Francis, in death also she followed the same road that he had taken.

The body was taken, feet first, carried by the prelates and followed by the whole Papal court, up the hill road and in through the Porta Nuova, while all the bells of Assisi rang out in her honour.

She was laid to rest in the church of St. George where the body of St. Francis had also been for two years. Always following him, the faithful woman was always with him: strong in poverty and in eternal glory.

And over that little church of St. George, a grand basilica had been built in her honour, splendid and spacious and called by her name — the Basilica of St. Clare.

First Edition, January 5, 1972
Printed in Italy at the
"Grafiche Messaggero di S. Antonio"
Basilica del Santo - Padua.